WILD THINGS!

Emu
on the loose

Lisa Regan
ILLUSTRATED BY **Kelly Byrne**

BLOOMSBURY
LONDON BERLIN NEW YORK SYDNEY

Published 2011 by
Bloomsbury Publishing PLC
49–51 Bedford Square, London, WC1B 3DP

www.bloomsbury.com

ISBN HB 978-1-4081-4247-9
      PB 978-1-4081-5678-0

Text copyright © 2010 Lisa Regan

The right of Lisa Regan to be identified as the author of this work has been asserted by her in accordance with the Copyrights, Designs and Patents Act 1988.

Manufactured and supplied under licence from the Zoological Society of London.
Copyright © 2011. All rights reserved.

A CIP catalogue for this book is available from the British Library.

All rights reserved. No part of this publication may be reproduced in any form or by any means – graphic, electronic or mechanical, including photocopying, recording, taping or information storage and retrieval systems – without the prior permission in writing of the publishers.

Every effort has been made to trace copyright holders and to obtain their permission for use of copyright material. The author and publishers would be pleased to rectify any error or omission in future editions.

This book is produced using paper that is made from wood grown in managed, sustainable forests. It is natural, renewable and recyclable. The logging and manufacturing processes conform to the environmental regulations of the country of origin.

Produced for Bloomsbury Publishing by Calcium. www.calciumcreative.co.uk

Illustrated by Kelly Bryne

Picture acknowledgements: Shutterstock: Sasha Davas 23tl, S.Cooper Digital 23tr.

Printed in China by Toppan Leefung

All the internet addresses given in this book were correct at the time of going to press. The author and publishers regret any inconvenience caused if addresses have changed or sites have ceased to exist, but can accept no responsibility for any such changes.

Contents

Ring, ring. Wild thing!	4
Zoom!	6
Big bird	8
Yuck	10
Play	12
Shiny	14
Splish!	16
Time to go home	18
Cool creatures	20
Glossary	22
ZSL London Zoo	23

Ring, ring. Wild thing!

If you're WILD about animals, today's your lucky day.

There's an emu at the door! You could invite it in...

4

Zoom!

Emus can't fly, but they are super-speedy.

An emu can run as fast as your car travels along a town street!

You will need

a **stopwatch**

trainers

to be very fit to keep up!

Big bird

Make some space! Emus are the second biggest bird in the world.

Emus can weigh up to 63 kilograms – that's the same weight as an adult!

You will need

a big sofa

more chairs

patient parents

Yuck

Feeding time could be interesting...

Emus eat fruit, **seeds**, **shoots**, insects, small animals – and even **droppings**.

You will need

a strong stomach

a long shopping list

Play

Emus love to play. They look as if they are dancing!

You will need

a lot of space

somewhere to hide when things get too rough

Shiny

Keep your sparkly things locked away.

You will need

a padlock and key

14

Splish!

Bath time may be a bit messy.

Emus love water. They paddle, sit in it and even put their head under.

You will need

a big bath

lots of bubbles

some bath toys

Time to go home

Your emu seems happy, but your parents really aren't!

It's time to post your pet back to its real home...

18

Cool creatures

Emus are from Australia.

Emus belong to the same **family** as **ostriches**. They are both types of bird that do not fly.

An adult emu can grow up to 1.9 metres tall. That's as big as a man!

A female emu can lay about ten eggs, but then leaves it to the father to look after the eggs and babies.

Emus have strong legs and sharp claws. They can give a mighty kick in order to **defend** themselves.

Flocks of emus will travel huge distances to find food.

Glossary

defend to protect
droppings animal poo
family a group of animals that are similar
flocks groups of birds that live together
ostriches very large birds that can run quickly but do not fly
resist to stop yourself doing something
seeds the small hard parts of plants from which new plants grow
shoots new plants that grow from the soil
stopwatch a watch that you can use to time how fast something moves

Thanks for having me!

The Zoological Society of London (ZSL) is a charity that provides help for animals at home and worldwide. We also run ZSL London Zoo and ZSL Whipsnade Zoo.

By buying this book, you have helped us raise money to continue our work with animals around the world.

Find out more at zsl.org

Take them all home!

ISBN   HB 978-1-4081-4247-9
         PB 978-1-4081-5678-0

ISBN   HB 978-1-4081-4246-2
         PB 978-1-4081-5679-7

ISBN   HB 978-1-4081-4245-5
         PB 978-1-4081-5680-3

ISBN   HB 978-1-4081-4244-8
         PB 978-1-4081-5681-0